sensual *self*

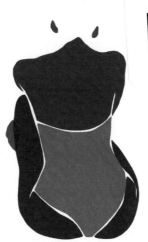

T0352873

*Prompts and Practices for
Getting in Touch with Your Body*

Ev'Yan Whitney

Clarkson Potter/Publishers
New York

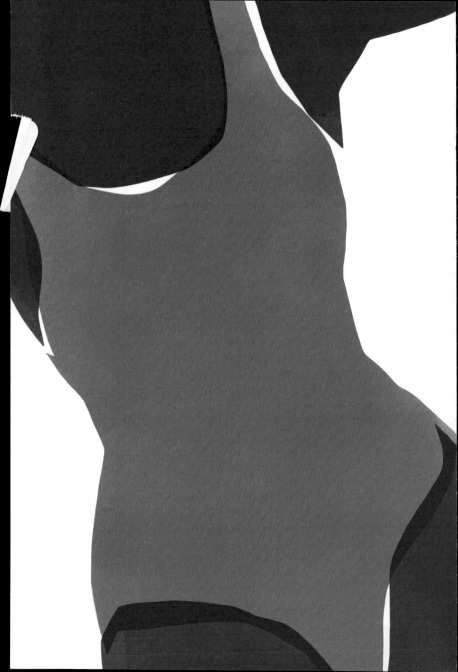

SENSUALITY HAS ALWAYS BEEN A VIBRANT FORCE in my life. For as long as I can remember, I've had a keen connection to my body and what I could do to make it feel good. Growing up in the Mojave Desert, my childhood was spent running around with my bare feet on the hot earth, sculpting cool, wet mud with my hands, and watching the dance of butterflies against the backdrop of desert sage. I cherished the moments I could be alone with my body, privately exploring its pleasure responses and finding freedom in this home that encouraged so much bliss. I didn't have language for what I was experiencing; it just was, and I trusted it.

I'd like to invite you to take a moment and pause with me.

I want you to imagine what it would feel like to be fully awake to your senses and the vital hum of your physical body. Imagine being able to trust and be fluent in the language of your body, and slowing down enough so that you can hear it clearly.

Let's go even deeper. Imagine having pleasure be the compass with which you navigate your day and the rhythm that guides you back home to your body. Imagine feeling completely comfortable in your own skin and having this inner confidence enhance the relationship you have with yourself and the world around you.

Who would you be in this new version of you? In a word, you would be **sensual.**

If you find yourself doubting whether walking through life in this sensual way is possible for you, you're not alone. We live at such a fast pace that it's often hard to tune into our own needs or notice that we even have a body. We forget to breathe. We forget to pause. We forget to feel. And when we do feel—either because we finally made the time or because our body demanded it—it's only for a fleeting moment.

Though this might be the age-old paradigm we've navigated the world with, many of us can sense that the distraction and disconnection from our sensual selves is not how it's supposed to be. We can sense that we're meant for more ease, enjoyment, and embodiment in our lives—we just don't know how to make living by that slow, sensual energy a reality.

We may live in a culture that values fast over slow, logic over feeling, rigidity over fluidity, mind over body, and we may have grown used to the repeated rituals of neglect, denial, repression, and disregard of our bodies, but we don't have to subscribe to that. We can choose to empower ourselves and engage in practices that give us more space to feel pleasure and joy as a way of liberating and healing ourselves.

Sensual Self is your first step on the path to reconnecting with and radically reclaiming your sensuality.

Let's walk it together.

WHO AM I?

MY NAME IS EV'YAN WHITNEY, AND I'VE WORKED as a Sexuality Doula and sex educator for over a decade. The first time I heard the word *sensual,* it was wrongly associated with sex and a specific performance of sexiness— a come-hither look, the swishing of hips, a lip bitten in desire. This notion of sensuality, combined with the negative messages I received about sex and my own body, created a harmful narrative in my mind that sensuality was not only bad, it also didn't belong to me. It belonged to the gazes of those who watched me perform it.

As I grew older, the sensual moments I experienced in my youth faded and were replaced with harmful falsehoods: my body was a temptation to myself and others, pleasure was a pathway to sin, and desire was a voice that should never be trusted. From these messages, my sensuality became weaponized. Exploring and occupying space with my body was no longer a harmless expression of my sensuality.

Now, I was being called "fast." If I yielded to any nudges my body gave me to pause and feel good, I was deemed self-centered or lazy. My body became a place of fear and shame, and pleasure was vilified.

As I've worked with clients and students over the years, I've heard similar stories. Body shame and disconnection from pleasure have been passed down and deeply ingrained within us by culture, religion, societal pressures, and trauma. As their guide and teacher, I help folks reclaim their connection to their bodies and their unique sensual and sexual identities on their own terms.

Sensual liberation and body reclamation won't happen overnight; this process takes patience, healing, and practice. But coming back to our sensuality is as necessary as it is rewarding.

WHAT EXACTLY IS SENSUALITY?

SENSUALITY IS THE PROCESS OF BEING CONNECTED to your body, your senses, and what makes you feel good. It's about seeking out pleasurable moments and, when that pleasure is found, inviting your whole body to savor it. More than anything, sensuality is about being present with your physical body and aware of how it interacts with the world. One of my favorite ways to think of sensuality is as the practice of paying attention with your senses.

If you've ever eaten a juicy piece of fruit and found yourself closing your eyes to savor each succulent bite, if you've been outside and stopped suddenly to drink in the sweet scent of a flower, if you've ever listened to music and felt your body begin to move with the beat without prompting— you have had a sensual experience. For a lot of us, these experiences are often short-lived, but sensuality is meant to be more than a fleeting moment. It's a practice that we have to nurture and a lifestyle we must choose to prioritize because sensuality, and the pleasure that comes from it, is our birthright.

You don't need to be taught how to be sensual; sensuality is inherently within you and you can access it at any time. You just need to reclaim it as yours—which is what this journal will help you do, step-by-step.

To be sensual, I think, is to respect
and rejoice in the force of life,
of life itself, and to be present *in* all
that one does, from the effort of loving
to the breaking of bread.

James Baldwin, *The Fire Next Time*

A WORD ON SEX, PLEASURE, AND SENSUALITY

ONE IMPORTANT THING YOU SHOULD KNOW
about sensuality: it's not synonymous with sexuality.
Sensuality stands on its own; it has its own identity,
experience, and expression—just as sexuality does. And
while everyone isn't sexual, everyone *is* sensual. If you
have a body, you are a sensual being, no matter what your
body looks like, is able to do, or your gender expression.
Sensuality is an intrinsic part of being human.

A lot can be said about how sensuality and sexuality
work in harmony, but that's not what this journal is
about. *Sensual Self* is about creating a basic and ongoing
connection with your body and your senses in a pleasurable
way, outside the experience of sex. Once we understand
that sex is not the only place we can access sensuality, an
entire world of possibility and pleasure opens up to us.

One underlying intention of sensuality is pleasure. Pleasure
is deeply rooted in sensuality; there cannot be one without
the other. But not all pleasure is sexual. We can (and often
do) experience pleasure in a plethora of what I call platonic

ways, but many of us are more familiar with pleasure within a sexual context and we often only give ourselves permission to access it during sex. Sexual pleasure is great, but we do ourselves and our bodies a disservice by seeing pleasure through that lens only. My hope is that through this journal you'll begin to explore your pleasure potential outside the bedroom.

All that said, it would be a huge oversight if I, a Sexuality Doula, didn't acknowledge or encourage a little curiosity around the juiciness that can be found within the sensual and the sexual. For many of us, our sexuality is just as fraught and overlooked as our sensuality, and, in the spirit of healing and liberation, it feels appropriate to bring some gentle exploration to our sexuality in this space, too. Just as pleasure and sensuality are inextricably linked, sexuality and sensuality are deeply intertwined. It's a beautiful serendipity that by reclaiming and embodying our sensuality we are better able to reclaim and embody our sexuality.

For some, sexual liberation is enmeshed with sensual liberation. In this journal you will find prompts that gently touch on your sexuality. If that makes you nervous, you're welcome to come back to those prompts later, but know that *Sensual Self* is designed to meet you where you are; every sensual, pleasurable thing you want is on the other side of fear.

HOW TO USE THIS JOURNAL

THIS JOURNAL WILL HELP YOU BEGIN A RITUAL of embodied sensuality. Each day that you connect with this journal, you'll begin to awaken sleeping parts of yourself and explore new ways of seeing and experiencing your body.

As you work through *Sensual Self,* you'll be given thoughtful questions and exercises that are intended to soften you, tune you into your senses, and gently examine anything that is in the way of you being fully present. With each prompt, you'll be asked to slow down, get quiet, and check in with yourself so that you can explore the unique expression of your sensuality without judgment.

Sensuality is a central theme of this journal, but because sensuality is deeply connected to many other things—how we see ourselves, the space we allow our bodies to occupy, how we express ourselves—you will encounter prompts on topics ranging from body acceptance to mindfulness and self-care. Some of the prompts will be questions that you answer journal-style, while others will invite you to complete an activity and put sensuality into action.

You can work through these prompts front to back, or you can randomly pick a prompt that ignites your curiosity that day. Sensuality isn't rigid or formulaic, and neither is this journal, so find your flow and trust it.

Most important, respect your process. If you find yourself hurrying through a prompt or feeling obligated to come to this journal, reconnect with your intentions. If you're not able to get there that day, that's okay. Take a break and come back when you can give yourself your full attention.

And if there is ever a prompt that you're unable to complete, feel free to skip it or interpret it in a way that feels more accessible for you.

YOUR INTENTIONS FOR THIS JOURNAL

BEFORE YOU BEGIN, IT'S IMPORTANT TO CONSIDER how you'd like to engage in this work and with what energy.

What intentions would you like to set as you work through this journal? What do you hope to learn about yourself? What do you hope to reclaim within yourself?

Use the following lines to write your intentions, and come back to these pages when you need to be reminded of why you're doing this important work.

SOME QUICK TIPS
BEFORE YOU BEGIN

TO GET THE MOST out of this experience, I suggest working through this journal a few times a week, if not daily. Also, consider designating a special time of day or a specific day (or days) of the week where you work through these prompts to help you stay consistent.

CREATE A MINI RITUAL before diving in. Put on something comfortable, turn on some chill music, make a cup of tea, do some light stretching, light a candle, and/or take a mindful breath or two before you get started on a new prompt.

FREE-WRITE your first thoughts first. Don't spend too much time trying to be eloquent or poetic. Just let the words flow and try not to judge what you're writing.

IF YOU GET STUMPED or triggered, always feel free to skip that prompt and come back to it later. Be kind to yourself.

KEEP WHAT YOU UNCOVERED in a prompt with you by writing a sentence or a word that stuck out to you and putting it on a sticky note for you to see throughout the day.

ENGAGE IN SELF-CARE as you work with these prompts. There are some questions that will likely bring up some strong emotions. So after you've written for the day, drink some water, take a bath, go for a walk, or make space to feel your feelings. Self-care is sensual.

*Sensuality does not wear
a watch but she always gets
to the essential places on time.
She is adventurous and not
particularly quiet.
She was reprimanded in
grade school because she
couldn't sit still all day long.
She needs to move.
She thinks with her body.*

J. Ruth Gendler, *The Book of Qualities*

My deepest hope is that *Sensual Self* will be a safe place for you to discover yourself; that you will begin to know yourself intimately, trust your body deeply, and become more literate in the language of your desires.

May the pleasure in your life increase. May the connection to your body strengthen. May you find delight and self-pride as you witness yourself becoming softer, freer, and more present through the practice of sensuality.

It is my honor and pleasure to help you find your way back to your sensual self.

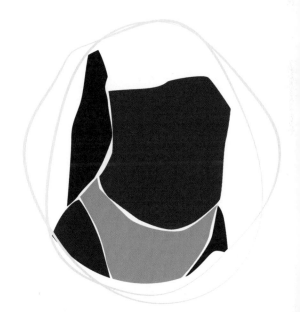

__/__/__

Think of a moment in your childhood when you felt completely free, joyous, safe, and fully in your body. Maybe you were in a state of play with yourself outside, or gardening with your grandparents, or helping a parent cook a meal. When you think of that moment, what were you doing? What were you feeling, hearing, eating, smelling, tasting, seeing? Who else was part of this moment? What emotions come up in your body as you invoke this memory? Use the lines below to write about the magic of that moment.

__/__/__

What do you need today in order to feel nourished?
(Examples: Do you need rest? To eat some vegetables?
To go outside? To wash your hair?)

GOING DEEPER

Do one or two of these things to bring nourishment to your day.

__/__/__

What do you want sensuality to mean to you? How would you like it to feel? Tap into your body's inherent wisdom about what sensuality is and write your own affirming definition that doesn't include any of the negative connotations culture has imposed on you.

In what ways do you keep your sensuality hidden? Why? What would it look like to courageously and boldly express your sensuality?

When we are embodied, we are totally present to our body and our senses. When was the last time you were completely aware of and in your body? What were you doing? Who were you with? How did you feel inside your body? Write a detailed description of this memory.

List five words that describe the relationship you currently have with your body—the way you think about it, the way you speak about it, the way you allow (or do not allow) it to occupy space.

1. _____

2. _____

3. _____

4. _____

5. _____

Now list five words that describe the relationship you would like to have with your body—how you'd like to see it, how you'd like to treat it, and how you'd like to honor it.

1. _____

2. _____

3. _____

4. _____

5. _____

As you step into your sensuality, you'll need to identify and let go of any blocks or old stories that are keeping you from body awareness and acceptance. What things seem to trigger you disliking, judging, criticizing, and/or comparing your body to others'? List anything (habits, people, media, limiting beliefs) that stop you from accepting your body as it is.

Which modern technologies tend to distract and disconnect you from your body and your senses? How do they distract you?

___/___/___

Play with your sense of touch today. Explore the world with touch, using your hands, feet, or face to feel all the different textures (bumpy and smooth), sensations (wet, oily, soft), and temperatures (hot, cold, lukewarm) that can be experienced. Write down everything that you touched and list all the sensations you felt in your body as you explored.

Sensuality lives and thrives in the moments when we slow down and become aware of the present moment. Where do you need to slow down? And what will you do today to remind yourself to move more slowly and mindfully?

_____

_____

_____

_____

_____

_____

_____

_____

_____

_____

_____

_____

_____

_____

_____

_____

_____

Think of someone (real or fictional) who exudes sensuality and total body confidence. What traits does this person possess that feel sensual to you? What is it about the way they carry themselves and claim space with their bodies? Jot down these characteristics and mannerisms.

Name five desires that are currently living in your body—big or small.

1. _____

2. _____

3. _____

4. _____

5. _____

What will you do today to get close to indulging at least one of those desires?

_____

_____

_____

_____

_____

_____

_____

__ / __ / __

If your energy in this moment were a color, what color would it be? If you want to change your energy, what color would you rather it be?

} *GOING DEEPER*

Wear something today in the color you want your energy to be.

Your sexuality is how you identify and express yourself as a sexual person. List at least five words or phrases that immediately come to mind when you think about your sexuality.

1. _____

2. _____

3. _____

4. _____

5. _____

Now choose one of those words or phrases and go deeper. Why do you think you associated that word or phrase to your sexuality? Write it down.

_____

_____

_____

_____

_____

_____

_____

___/___/___

Finish this sentence: I love my body when it is . . .

In a sexual context, how do you want to be touched in order to experience pleasure? How do you want to be kissed? Cuddled? Caressed? Write it all down and allow yourself to want what you want.

_____

_____

_____

_____

_____

_____

_____

_____

_____

_____

_____

GOING DEEPER

Masturbation is a great way to explore your sexual wants and needs. If you're comfortable, self-pleasure today and pay close attention to what makes you feel good and the specifics of those actions. Are your touches light or firm? Do you like to play with a little pain or prefer it without? What parts of your body do you tend to steer clear of and why? Use masturbation as a reference to help you understand what your body needs to feel good during sex.

What does an enthusiastic "yes!" feel like in your body? What sensations or signals come up in your body that affirm this "yes"? If it helps, reflect on a previous time when your body was giving you an enthusiastic "yes."

Who first taught you about sensuality and feeling good in your own body? What did they teach you?

_____

_____

_____

_____

_____

_____

_____

_____

_____

_____

_____

_____

_____

_____

_____

_____

_____

_____

GOING DEEPER

If you're comfortable with it, thank them for being a teacher and advocate for your pleasure and sensuality.

___/___/___

Nature is a beautiful source of sensual inspiration. By witnessing the timeless beauty of trees, plants, and animals, we become reconnected with ourselves and the magic of the world around us. Go outside today and notice all the things you see, smell, touch, feel, and/or hear that arouse your senses. Gaze up at trees, feel your feet being supported by the ground, attune your ears to the sounds you hear, observe the many different colors around you, stop and smell flowers, and trail your fingers across different textures. After your time outside, come to this page and reflect on what you experienced.

GOING DEEPER

Consider leaving your phone at home and bring this journal with you instead, jotting down everything in real time.

How do you want to feel today, both emotionally and physically? How can you make those feelings a reality?

__ / __ / __

Explore with your sense of taste today. Give your undivided attention to at least one meal and with every bite, pause to savor the taste of your food. Chew slowly. Try to pinpoint specific flavors and textures. After you've finished eating, give thanks to your body for processing food into energy and nourishment. How was this experience of slow eating and savoring different from the ways you usually eat a meal?

GOING DEEPER

After you've eaten, take a moment to thank your body for its ability to process food and turn it into energy and nourishment.

Pleasure is the feeling of doing something that makes you feel good while fully enjoying that experience. Write down all the things that make you feel good and give you non-sexual pleasure.

"Let there be pleasure and ecstasy on earth and let it begin with me."

Annie Sprinkle, interview in *Hartford Courant*

__/__/__

What hardens your body and makes it tense? *(Examples: loud sounds, when someone crosses a boundary, feeling obligated to do something that doesn't bring you joy.)*

What softens your body and helps it relax? *(Examples: listening to your favorite song, drinking a glass of wine, sitting in a hot bath, being around your loved ones.)*

Body check-in: If your body could speak to you at this moment, what would it say?

It may be difficult to practice sensuality if you make judgments and feel resentful of your body. Let's make some space to explore body acceptance. What parts of your body need more of your love and acceptance? Why are you critical of those parts? What could you say to/about your body to help you feel neutral or accepting of it?

What emotions tend to be the hardest for you to feel and accept? Why? What are some alternate ways you could meet and respond to these emotions?

___/___/___

Senses check-in: Name three things you hear in this moment.

1.

2.

3.

Explore your sense of sight today. Take an object in the room you're in or look at what's happening outside the window and study it. Look at the colors, textures, shapes, shadows, and layers of depth. Now describe it in vivid detail.

GOING DEEPER

After you've finished writing, take out a new piece of paper and try your hand at drawing what you see. Try to capture the textures, shapes, and colors as you see and experience them.

___ / ___ / ___

Desire is not just sexual. It's a signal that our body gives us to go in the direction of pleasure and soothing. One word that's associated with desire is *craving,* which is often attached to food and eating, but can also apply to the experience of your whole body. What is your body craving right now? Write it all down, big or small.

) *GOING DEEPER*
} If you have the ability to indulge in one or all of these cravings safely and
(consensually, go for it!

Which of your senses is your favorite? Write a little love letter to that sense, telling it why.

Dear _____,

_____

_____

_____

_____

_____

_____

_____

_____

_____

_____

_____

_____

Love,

_____

__/__/__

What physical sensations do you notice in your belly right now?
Describe them in detail.

If sensuality were a time of day, what time of day would it be? Why?

___/___/___

Make an altar to sensuality today. Claim a corner in your home and collect things that bring delight to your senses, remind you to soften, and inspire you to be present in your body.
(Examples: a bowl of sticky honey, sweet smelling flowers, glitter, feathers, crystals, moss, candles, incense, a photo of yourself or a photo of a person or deity who inspires your sensuality.)

Every time you pass your altar, take a moment to pause and reflect. Envision who you're becoming and what you'd like to deepen within your practice of sensuality. Let this altar remind you of how sensual you are.

GOING DEEPER

Make a practice of interacting with your altar daily. Pause to use the items to awaken your senses and let this altar be a designated space to help you connect to pleasure and your sensual body.

What external appearance or state have you tried to conform your body to before you could start loving it? Why? *(Examples: weight loss, weight gain, clearer skin, longer hair, etc.)* Reflect on the ways you've imposed certain shoulds on your body, and why.

___ / ___ / ___

Pick a specific area of your life (your work, home, relationships, creativity, spirituality, sexuality) that needs more ease. What would that look like? How would more ease change the way you operate in this part of your life?

Ground yourself in this moment. Wherever you are, place your feet on the ground (or sink deeply into your seat) and feel it stabilizing, supporting, and rooting you. Pause here, close your eyes, and breathe. What does it feel like to be grounded?

GOING DEEPER

Come back to this practice whenever you feel yourself spinning and need to reconnect with your body and the environment around you.

We have more than five senses. Our sixth sense, our intuition, is a vital part of being human. It's also an ally to our sensuality and body. What is your relationship with your intuition like? Do you listen to it? Do you trust it? When do you tend to neglect or dismiss it most?

On a scale of 1 to 5, 1 being not at all connected and 5 being totally connected, how connected do you feel to your body right now? Why did you choose that number?

_____

_____

_____

_____

_____

_____

_____

_____

_____

_____

_____

_____

_____

_____

What consistently brings you joy? What steals your joy away? In what areas of your life do you feel you need to reclaim your joy?

Write about a time when you felt completely safe in and totally trusting of your body. What did that safety and trust feel like?

GOING DEEPER

What specifically does your body need from you to feel safe today? Does it need you to give it more comfort? More quiet? More self-care? Set the intention to bring more safety to your body by giving your body what it needs.

One of the biggest culprits that can keep us disconnected from our sensuality is being too much in our own head. It's hard to quiet the hum of our busy minds, and restless thoughts prevent us from being fully present in our body. When you get stuck in your head, where does your mind go? What thoughts make you spiral? In moments when you're thinking too much, what does your mind need in order to quiet down?

Take a moment to tune into your body and name three sensations that you notice—maybe a gurgling stomach, goose bumps, a hot flash, muscle spasms, or pain. Make note of where these sensations are living in your body. If these sensations each had their own voice, what would they be trying to communicate to you?

___/___/___

If your sensuality were an animal, which animal would it be?

) *GOING DEEPER*

Do some research on this particular animal today. Learn about its characteristics, how it lives, how it moves, how it provides for itself, how it mates. Try embodying the essence of that animal to inspire your own sensuality.

Do you experience any shame or fear when it comes to your sexuality? What negative narratives are you carrying that keep you from feeling free in your sexual expression? Where do you think that shame comes from?

Close your eyes and take a couple of conscious breaths. Next, scan your whole body, starting from the top of your head, to your shoulders, to your hands, to your belly, to your thighs, to your knees, to your feet. Take note of where you feel tension in your body. Place a hand on the part of your body where you felt most tense, and tune into it. What does that tension need in order to be released?

*"Give your body an hour a day.
If it's not worth an hour a day,
there's nothing your body can tell you
and not much else anyone can do."*

Marion Woodman, *Coming Home to Myself*

What acts of self-care would you like to engage in to give your body some love? Set aside one hour that's meant to be just for you and your body—maybe take a hot bath, give yourself a gentle massage, have a solo dance party, or simply allow your body to rest. Now put your phone on DO NOT DISTURB and give your body your undivided attention for an hour.

GOING DEEPER

Often when we give ourselves and our bodies our undivided attention, our inner critic can pop up and try to shame us for taking some much-needed Me Time. While indulging in intentional self-care today, make note of where your mind goes and how it tries to get you to disregard this time you're taking for yourself.

__/ __/ __

Put your hand on your heart. Inhale your breath and exhale it slowly, closing your eyes. How's your heart today? How's your breath? Respond to these questions from the perspective of both your heart and your breath.

Body check-in: Take a moment to ask your body what it needs from you today. What's coming up? What might need to be shifted around for those needs to be met?

Write about a time when you denied your body the pleasure it wanted—perhaps it was dark chocolate, snuggling with your partner, playing hooky, or allowing someone to take care of you. What do you think would've happened if you had indulged in that pleasure?

What are some old stories or limiting beliefs you have about your ability to be sensual? And what new stories or positive affirmations do you want to replace them with?

Finish this sentence: I feel my most sensual when . . .

One of the fastest ways to be reminded of our body and our senses is through gratitude. When we take a moment to pause and appreciate the little things, like the warm sun hitting our skin or water that quenches our thirst, we have no choice but to connect to our senses and our surroundings. What small, simple things are you grateful for in this moment?

___/___/___

What kind of relationship do you have to your belly—the look of it, the feel of it, what it craves? Do you wish your belly looked different? Occupied less space? Didn't have so many needs? What kind of relationship do you want to have with your belly instead? Write a letter to your belly—both apologizing for the judgments you may have imposed upon it and extending it gratitude so that you can begin to heal this relationship.

Write down five ways you would like to embody and celebrate your sensuality. Then, say them aloud to yourself as affirmations. An example: "I want to embody my sensuality with ease" turns into the affirmation "I embody my sensuality with ease." Say them even if you haven't achieved it yet—not only because our words have power but because you are in the process of accomplishing these sensual goals.

1. _____

_____

2. _____

_____

3. _____

_____

4. _____

_____

5. _____

_____

__/_/__

Do something nice for yourself today that'll arouse and inspire your senses. Buy yourself some flowers, put on your favorite scent, make yourself the perfect cup of tea, or adorn your body with clothing, jewelry, or makeup that makes you feel like royalty. Luxuriate in how it feels to be good to your sensual body.

Play with your sense of smell today. Explore the different smells you come across, particularly the ones you don't normally notice. Take deep breaths and fill your lungs with the smells of your home, the food you eat, the natural world outside, and your own body. List all the scents you came across and see if you can describe the nuances of their fragrance. *(Examples: peppery, airy sweet, sharp, musky.)*

If your sensuality were a color (or colors), which would it be?

When you're feeling overtaxed, anxious, or fatigued, how does your body want to be soothed? What's your favorite way to bring comfort and relaxation to your body?

___/___/___

What does a firm "no" feel like in your body? What sensations or signals come up that let you know your body doesn't want to do something?

Reflect on all the ways your body has been there for you—from getting you where you need to go to helping you express yourself to digesting your food. What does your body do for you without your asking?

_____

_____

_____

_____

_____

_____

_____

_____

_____

_____

_____

_____

_____

_____

_____

_____

GOING DEEPER

Write your body a quick thank-you note for all that it does for you.

Being vulnerable is one example of letting yourself be soft. Write about a recent time you were vulnerable with somebody. In what ways did you reveal your tenderness to them? What emotions came up for you? What physical sensations?

Sensuality requires that you not only know yourself and your body, but that you trust yourself. Where do you need to trust yourself more? What tends to undermine that trust? What actions can you take to reinstill that trust?

__ / __ / __

Senses check-in: Name three things you smell in this moment.

1. _____

_____

_____

2. _____

_____

_____

3. _____

_____

_____

List all your favorite physical features and body parts.
Why do you love them?

__ / __ / __

Who are you when you are playful? Are there noticeable changes to your characteristics, mannerisms, or the way you inhabit your body? Jot them down.

What's the look, feel, and vibe of the kind of sex you'd like to have? What words would you use to describe it? How do you want to feel when you're having this kind of sex? How do you want your senses and body to be activated? How would you like your partner to engage with you? And what would you need to feel safe to have this kind of sex?

__ / __ / __

Finish this sentence: Right now, my mind needs . . .

What bodily functions do you tend to suppress? *(Examples: yawning, burping, farting, holding your bladder.)* Why? How do you want to meet these needs instead of holding them in?

) ***GOING DEEPER***
} Commit to allowing your body the freedom to express and release itself as it
(needs to today.

__/__/__

For one hour today, put away your phone and other digital devices and engage in an activity that you usually would've done with the help of modern technology. Read a book and notice the way the pages feel on your fingertips. Write a letter to a friend and pay attention to the way your own handwriting looks. Eat dinner by candlelight. Wash your dishes by hand. Afterward, come back and answer this question: How much more sensual was your experience without modern technology?

What fears, anxieties, or insecurities do you have about outwardly exploring and expressing your sensuality?

_____

_____

_____

_____

_____

_____

_____

_____

_____

_____

_____

_____

_____

_____

_____

Body check-in: If your body were one of the four elements—
water, earth, fire, air—which would it be today? Why?

Pause and check in. What is one emotion you are experiencing right now? Can you pinpoint where this emotion is living in your body? What sensations does it create in your body? And if you were to ask this emotion what it needs from you in order to feel accepted, what would it say?

Take a look around your home. What can you do to make your home more pleasing to your senses? What needs to be brought in? What needs to be taken out?

Which of your senses tends to get less of your attention? Which of your senses do you tend to take for granted?

_____

_____

_____

_____

_____

_____

_____

_____

_____

_____

_____

_____

_____

_____

_____

_____

_____

} *GOING DEEPER*

Give this sense more of your attention today and make an effort to engage with it a little more.

___ / ___ / ___

Use this page to create a piece of art that is an ode to your sensuality. It can be a drawing, a poem, a collage, or anything else you can imagine.

"We have it in us to be splendid. "

Maya Angelou

What daily habits do you have that tend to disconnect you from your body and senses? What new habits would you like to adopt to help you stay more physically embodied and sensually aware?

__ / __ / __

If sensuality were a song, which one would it be? Why did you choose that song?

GOING DEEPER

Make a playlist of songs that inspire your sensuality and the feeling of fully being in your body.

Describe your last orgasm in five words.

1. _____

2. _____

3. _____

4. _____

5. _____

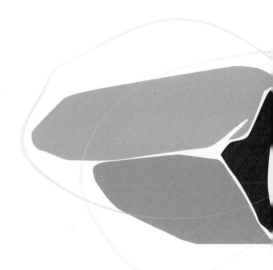

"An orgasm a day keeps the doctor away."

Mae West

__/__/__

Holding space is the process of showing up and giving emotional presence to someone when they're in need of support. Many of us are familiar with holding space for others, but we very rarely hold space for ourselves. Think of a recent time where you've held space for someone else. How did you show up for this person emotionally and/or physically? What would it look like for you to provide yourself with the same support?

Name any hard feelings that are present for you in this moment—
stress, self-criticism, judgment, anxiety, fear. What happened recently
(or currently) that is bringing up these emotions?

> *GOING DEEPER*
>
> We tend to run away from challenging emotions, often because they're
> uncomfortable to face. As you bring some gentle awareness to these
> feelings, take in a deep breath and visualize that your breath is softening
> the edges of those emotions and creating space, however small, for other
> lighter emotions.

___/___/___

Write an open letter to your body. What do you want it to know?
What do you want to express to your body?

Dear _____,

Love,

_____

What does sensual sex look like? Feel like? Sound like?
Paint a detailed picture with words.

Explore your sense of hearing today. Put on your headphones and play one of your favorite songs, only this time, close your eyes and focus on it. Listen to the beat, the instrumentals, the vocals, the lyrics. Observe any emotions or sensations that come up in your body as you tune into the sounds—goose bumps, joy, inspiration, heat, a memory. How different did the song sound this time? What new things did you notice about the song?

There can be no sensual embodiment without total acceptance of our bodies as they imperfectly are—including what our bodies look like when they're unclothed. No matter what the state of your body, no matter what negative narratives have been imposed upon it, your body is a sensual body. This exercise will help you develop a new level of radical acceptance of it.

Take off all your clothes and stand in front of a mirror. Set a timer for three minutes and take in your reflection. If you start trying to define or judge what you see, take an intentional slow inhale for a count of five and exhale for a count of five. Repeat this two more times. As the timer ticks down, observe your body—its curves, scars, shadows, and its different pigments and textures—objectively without imposing any opinions or "shoulds" on it. See if you can let your body be a body for a couple of minutes.

What emotions or sensations came up as you did this exercise?

_____

_____

_____

_____

_____

_____

_____

_____

GOING DEEPER
Revisit this exercise whenever you want to connect with your naked body.

Think back to the last time you enjoyed sex. What did you like about it? How did your body feel? Is there something you would've changed about that experience—either on your part or on the part of your sexual partner, or both?

Body check-in: How have you been feeling in your body since you began exploring your sensuality? When did you notice the change?

What does fear feel like in your body? What does joy feel like in your belly? What does sadness feel like in your chest? Write down the sensations that accompany these emotions and where you feel them in your body.

As you explore your sensual self, it's important to set boundaries to keep your sensuality engaged and in focus even amid the endless distractions of social media, the news, difficult people, and the frenetic energy of the world around us.

What boundaries do you need to put into place to prioritize your sensual energy? Having a dedicated time of day free of devices? Putting a time limit on social media? Advocating for more sensual energy within your relationships? Creating a morning ritual that begins your day with sensual intention? Brainstorm what boundaries you want to set.

_____

_____

_____

_____

_____

_____

_____

_____

_____

_____

_____

_____

_____

If your sensuality were personified into a person, what character traits would they have? How would they dress? How would they talk? How would they walk? What would they do for work? What would their lovers be like? What kind of relationship would they have with their body? Create a character profile.

_____

_____

_____

_____

_____

_____

_____

_____

_____

_____

_____

_____

_____

_____

_____

_____

_____

_____

_____

_____

What affirmations do you want to say to (and embody in) yourself to advocate for more sensual energy within your relationships?

The erotic is a measure between our sense of self and the chaos of our strongest feelings. It is an internal sense of satisfaction to which, once we have experienced it, we know we can aspire. For having experienced the fullness of this depth of feeling . . . we can require no less of ourselves.

Audre Lorde, _Uses of the Erotic_

List five things you would like to do to be good to yourself today.

1. _____

_____

2. _____

_____

3. _____

_____

4. _____

_____

5. _____

_____

What have you done to your body—intentionally or unintentionally—that you need to forgive yourself for? Write down any boundaries you've crossed, any pressures you've put on yourself, or any negative ways you've denied your body what it needs.

GOING DEEPER

Make amends by writing a letter to your body and asking for its forgiveness. As you write, don't focus all your attention on guilt. Instead, speak to what you've learned and how different your actions will be moving forward.

Place a hand on your chest. Without changing your current breathing pattern, what is the state of your breathing? What do you notice about your breaths? Are they shallow? Do they live in your chest or do they come from your belly? Are you subconsciously holding your breath?

Now that you've brought some awareness to your breathing, take an intentional, slow inhale of your breath for a count of five and exhale for a count of five. Repeat this two more times. Now check in again: Do you feel any different?

What emotional clutter is
causing you to disconnect from
pleasure?

_____

_____

_____

_____

_____

_____

_____

_____

_____

_____

_____

_____

_____

_____

_____

_____

__ / __ / __

Finish this sentence: My senses are the most activated and engaged when I am . . .

It's not often that we allow ourselves to sit in silence. We're constantly busying ourselves, either because there always seems to be something that needs our attention or we're uncomfortable with being still. Set a timer for three minutes and do nothing. Just sit in silence and observe.

How was it to sit still? Where did your mind go? What feelings or emotions came up for you while sitting still?

GOING DEEPER

As you're sitting in silence, your mind will likely go in many different directions. If you notice your mind racing, try bringing your focus back to your breathing to help come back to the present.

Describe your sensuality—the energy of it, the essence of it, the look and feel of it, and how you express it.

Coming home to yourself is the process of not only being comfortable and grounded in your body, it's also about trusting the personal history, sensations, needs, desires, and messages you and your body experience consistently. Do you feel at home within yourself? Why or why not? What would need to happen (or what things would need to change) in order for you to feel at home in your body?

_"Coming home to ourselves . . . reassures us that
we're meant to be here—messy, imperfect, and just as we are."_

Victoria Emanuela and Caitlin Metz, *My Body, My Home*

___/__/__

What acts of self-care would you like to practice each morning to help you start your day sensually embodied? And what acts of self-care would you like to practice to end your day mindfully? Write down at least two for each time of day. In doing so, you are creating a mini ritual.

AM

_____

_____

_____

_____

PM

_____

_____

_____

_____

} *GOING DEEPER*

Challenge yourself to put these rituals into practice tomorrow.

Senses check-in: Which of your senses do you notice the most in this moment? And which of your senses aren't being directly activated?

_____

_____

_____

_____

_____

_____

_____

_____

_____

_____

_____

_____

_____

_____

_____

_____

_____

_____

If your sensuality were a famous piece of art, which would it be? What is it about that piece that reminds you of your sensuality?

Pause and reflect. What is the dominant sensation in your body right now?

_____

_____

_____

_____

_____

_____

_____

_____

_____

_____

_____

_____

_____

_____

_____

_____

_____

___/___/___

When you think of the word *sensual*, what other words immediately come to mind? *(Examples: succulent, soft, pleasure, slow, confidence.)* Write some synonyms.

In a sexual context, what turns you on? And how do you know when you're turned on? What sensations come up in your body to let you know you're aroused?

If you get stuck, think back to the last pleasant sexual encounter you had and use that as a reference.

_____

_____

_____

_____

_____

_____

_____

_____

_____

_____

_____

_____

_____

_____

_____

GOING DEEPER

Now that you've given space to what turns you on, what turns you off?

Imagine yourself in the future as someone who has made sensuality a consistent practice in their life. Write a letter as this person to your current self. What does your future sensual self want you to know, based on where you currently are in your journey?

What does your sensual body require in order for it to feel good and comfortable on a daily basis? Soft, flexible fabric? Hot water with lemon? A fresh breeze through an open window? Music playing while you work? Write down at least five of these external needs.

1. _____

_____

2. _____

_____

3. _____

_____

4. _____

_____

5. _____

_____

What's your mental chatter like today? What thoughts need to be quieted, if any?

Body check-in: What movements or positions does your body want to be in to help it relax and soften in this moment?

GOING DEEPER

Ask this question periodically throughout the day and make an effort to make your body comfortable.

__/__/__

Write a poem or a haiku about your sensual body.

Who are you becoming sensually? What characteristics or traits are you noticeably embodying more often? How have your daily habits changed, if at all, to support your sensual self? Reflect on all the ways you are becoming a sensual being.

__ / __ / __

When it comes to your sensual body, what do you need more of?

What do you need less of?

Finish this sentence: I nourish my well-being by . . .

What parts of your life could use more playful energy? Your work life?
Your sex life? How different would these parts of your life
look if more play were incorporated?

Pick one part of your body—a hip, your belly, your left hand, your lips, the skin on your shoulder—and use a mirror to help you study it. On the following lines, write descriptive, neutral words as though you were describing this part of your body to someone who has never seen it before.

Intimacy is the experience of mutual friendship, vulnerability, affection, and emotional closeness with another. In what ways can you be intimate with yourself today?

Write down 10 of your secret desires. They can be things you want, experiences you want to have with others, or things you would like to do or feel for the pleasure of it.

1. _____

2. _____

3. _____

4. _____

5. _____

6. _____

7. _____

8. _____

9. _____

10. _____

__ / __ / __

Write five affirmations that speak to the healing and freedom you
would like to experience in your sexuality.

1.

2.

3.

4.

5.

GOING DEEPER

Write at least one of these affirmations on a sticky note and place it
somewhere in your home, so you can connect to it throughout the day.

Senses check-in: Name three textures you feel in this moment.

1.

2.

3.

When it comes to your sensuality, what have you been observing about yourself and your body lately? What have you been noticing about others and the way they inhabit (or don't inhabit) their bodies?

Finish this sentence: I feel the most comfortable in my body when . . .

___ / ___ / ___

Write down five demands or needs people regularly expect you to
fulfill that you would like to say no to.

1. _____

_____

2. _____

_____

3. _____

_____

4. _____

_____

5. _____

_____

Plan a day for yourself in which pleasure is the focus, you allow your sensual body to flow without ridigity, and your senses are considered every step of the way. Write out how you would like this day to unfold, from the time you wake up to when you go to sleep. Where would you go? What would you eat? How would you dress? What would you spend your time doing? And what energy would you like this day to be infused with?

___ / __ / __

In what ways do you think sensuality and sensual embodiment enhance your sexual experiences? List at least five ways.

1.

2.

3.

4.

5.

Pause and say this affirmation aloud to yourself: "I am a sensual being."

What thoughts or emotions immediately came up when you said this aloud?

_____

_____

_____

_____

_____

_____

_____

_____

_____

_____

_____

_____

GOING DEEPER

Sometimes when we say affirmations, the voice of our inner critic pipes up and says, "That's not true." Practice saying, "I am a sensual being" to yourself throughout the day and as you do, pay close attention to what that voice says to diminish or undercut your efforts to affirm yourself.

__ / __ / __

Choose a chore *(washing dishes, making your bed, doing laundry)* and give your full focus and attention to it today. Stay present to the entire process and pay attention to the sounds, smells, sights, sensations, and the way your body moves to perform the task. Bring your focus back to your breathing if you get distracted. Reflect on what you experienced and noticed while you were engaged in this chore.

List five things that dull your senses.

1. _____

2. _____

3. _____

4. _____

5. _____

Now list five things that delight your senses.

1. _____

2. _____

3. _____

4. _____

5. _____

Reflect on a time when you should've listened to your body, but you didn't. What was going on? If you could go back in time, what would you have done differently?

Finish this sentence: I know my intuition is speaking to me because it sounds like . . .

and feels like. . .

What does it feel like to be disconnected from your body? How does it make you act? How do you know when you're disconnected from your body? And where does that energy go instead?

_____

_____

_____

_____

_____

_____

_____

_____

_____

_____

_____

_____

_____

_____

_____

_____

_____

_____

What small and simple things can you do to bring yourself more pleasure and enjoyment today?

_____

_____

_____

_____

_____

_____

_____

_____

_____

_____

_____

_____

_____

_____

_____

_____

"Pleasure is the point.
Feeling good is not frivolous, it is freedom."

adrienne maree brown

__/__/__

How does your sensuality want to be expressed in this moment?
Reflect here.

Tune into the emotions and/or bodily sensations that are present for you right now. Use the lines below to name them without judgment. *(Examples: I am anxious, I am comfortable, I am sore.)* As you make space for those emotions and/or sensations, go through each one individually and ask it what it might need (either from you or from someone else) to be relieved.

_____

_____

_____

_____

_____

_____

_____

_____

_____

_____

_____

_____

GOING DEEPER

As you give your body and these emotions space to be what they are, take a moment to acknowledge them. Place a hand on your body and affirm yourself by saying, "I hear you."

__ / __ / __

What desires do you have that you need to communicate with your partner(s) in order for you to have more pleasurable, sensual sex with them?

What systems of oppression have policed your body and/or
your sensuality? In what ways has your sensuality and/or your
body been oppressed?

_____

_____

_____

_____

_____

_____

_____

_____

_____

_____

_____

_____

_____

_____

_____

} *GOING DEEPER*

Reflect on the steps you can take to begin to disentangle yourself from these
systems to the best of your ability.

___/___/___

Create a sensuality mood board. Get out some magazines and cut out images of nature scenes, art, plants, flowers, colors, animals, words, bodies, or anything else that is sensual to you, and glue them onto a poster board. After you've created it, come back to this page and write 10 words that describe the mood board you made.

1. _____

2. _____

3. _____

4. _____

5. _____

6. _____

7. _____

8. _____

9. _____

10. _____

GOING DEEPER

Put this mood board in a place where you'll always see it. Or take a photo of it and make it a wallpaper on your phone.

Name five things you're proud of when it comes to your body.

1. _____

_____

2. _____

_____

3. _____

_____

4. _____

_____

5. _____

_____

___/___/___

List the specific sights, sounds, tastes, smells, sensations, and things
you associate with winter, spring, summer, and fall.

WINTER

SPRING

SUMMER

FALL

Give your body some loving touch today—touch that is infused with an intention: love, acceptance, and kindness. After taking a shower and while your body is still slightly damp, work some body oil or lotion into your hands and massage it into your skin. While you're massaging yourself, say kind things to and about your body quietly to yourself.

Before this exercise, how were you feeling emotionally? Physically? How does your body and mind feel now?

"It is very important that we do not only see our bodies as places that can be harmed, but also as bodies capable of experiencing deep love, pleasure, and liberation."

Dalychia Saah and Rafaella Fiallo, creators of Afrosexology

Finish this sentence: My definition of *sexy* is . . .

If you were to create five new "rules" you'd like to live by to guide you and keep you consistent as you express your sensuality, what would those rules be? *(Examples: I will spend at least 30 minutes in nature each day; I will center my pleasure in everything I do; I will make space and time for the needs of my body.)* Think big!

1. _____

_____

2. _____

_____

3. _____

_____

4. _____

_____

5. _____

_____

__ / __ / __

When your body is overworked and exhausted, how does it feel?
What physical sensations come up in your body that let you know
you need to rest?

Take a sensual selfie today—a selfie that captures a moment in time where you are being present in your body, accentuating your softness and strength, and feeling confident in your own skin. Feel free to use props like flowers to help bring some sensual energy to the photo. Describe who you saw in that photo below—you can even paste the photo here.

GOING DEEPER

A sensual selfie is more of a mood or intention than a particular kind of photo. When you're about to take your selfie, think about the sensual being you are liberating and healing within yourself, how connected you are to your body, and the voice of your desires. Take a photo with the intention of capturing that essence. If it's helpful, go back to the intentions you wrote in the beginning and use them to inspire your pose, presence, and energy.

When was the last time you felt completely satisfied? What made you feel that way—a delicious meal? A good night's rest? A recent conversation with a friend? What does feeling satisfied feel like in your body?

Choose a part of your body—the top of your head, your pinky toe, your left elbow, the roof of your mouth—and bring conscious awareness to it. See if you can feel into that specific part of your body, isolating it from all others. Bring focus and awareness to the aliveness of this part of your body. What does that aliveness feel like? A warm buzz? A lightness? A weightedness? Describe that sensation in vivid detail.

Name five things that you enjoy the smell, taste, feel, sound, and/or sight of.

1.

2.

3.

4.

5.

What is something you would like to give to your body today?

What is something you would like to receive from your body today?

___/___/___

Finish this sentence: I feel most secure when . . .

Close your eyes. Breathe into your belly. Relax your jaw. Lower your shoulders. Soften your brow. Feel your feet on the ground, your back on your chair, or your body making contact with whatever it's resting on. Now that you've softened into your body, ask yourself: What do I need in this moment? Write down all your body's specific needs, from big to the small.

GOING DEEPER

What is stopping you from giving these specific needs to your body? If big things are coming up for you around giving in to your body's needs—shame, fear, judgment, self-doubt—take a breath and see if you can pinpoint where that voice is coming from. Next, choose one of your body's needs and indulge in it today. The more you give in to your body's needs without self-criticism, the easier this process will become.

Name five things you will commit to doing long term to keep your sensual self prioritized, nourished, and sacred.

1. _____

_____

2. _____

_____

3. _____

_____

4. _____

_____

5. _____

_____

FINAL REFLECTION

LOOK BACK AT SOME OF THE PROMPTS YOU COMPLETED.
How have you changed? How differently do you relate to your
body? To your senses? Reflect on your growth.

ACKNOWLEDGMENTS

Sensual Self was such a pleasure to write, and I hold much gratitude in my heart for those who aided and guided me as I wrote it. Gabrielle Van Tassel, thank you for your impeccable editorial eye and for being the spark that helped ignite this project, and a big thank you to the Clarkson Potter team who made this journal a reality. Célia Amroune and Aline Kpade, thank you for your gorgeous illustrative talents which made *Sensual Self* even more sensual and beautiful. Jonathan Mead, my husband, who has taught me so much about embodiment, movement, sensuality, vulnerability, healing, and pleasure: your unfaltering love and belief in me have kept me grounded. Lesley Asare, medicinal-mover, art-healer, and dearest friend—you were in my heart the entire time I was writing this. Simone Dankenbring, my mother: thank you for fostering my creative, sensual spirit and for instilling in me the gift of expressing myself through writing. And to my ancestors: for every risk you took in service of your sovereignty, for every unignored desire you ever felt, for every fleeting moment you experienced freedom and pleasure in your own body—this is in honor of you. Thank you for speaking to and through me as I weaved healing and power with my words. I love you.

The writing of this journal was fueled and inspired by the following sensual pleasures:

SOUNDS Alice Coltrane, Dave Brubeck, Thievery Corporation, Mndsgn, Pharoah Sanders, Toro y Moi, Washed Out, Mulatu Astatke, and the church bells that toll in my neighborhood on the hour.

TASTES Green smoothies; freshly baked chocolate almond croissants from my local farmers' market; rich, buttery decaf coffee; juicy summer fruits; and clean water.

SIGHTS Candlelight, yellow hibiscus, reflections of the sun hitting my dining room windows; and all of my gorgeous plant housemates.

SMELLS Frankincense resin; Van Van oil; dried *Craspedia*; lavender and eucalyptus; and my dog Sofie's familiar, earthy scent.

FEELINGS The feel of airy cotton caftans and brightly colored robes on my body; the weight of gold on my fingers and around my neck; the warm sun on my skin; the cool wind blowing through my curtains; and being held by hot water in my bathtub when my mind/body needed a reset.

Ev'Yan Whitney is a Sexuality Doula and somatics practitioner whose work focuses on decolonizing and unshaming sexuality at the intersection of identity, pleasure, and embodiment. She is a sensual dance meditation facilitator and hosts the podcast *Sensual Self*.